Bernie Bee's Wings Won't Work

©This edition published 2023. First published in 2022.
BookLife Publishing Ltd.
King's Lynn, Norfolk, PE30 4LS, UK

ISBN 978-1-80155-145-8

All rights reserved. Printed in Poland.
A catalogue record for this book is available
from the British Library.

Bernie Bee's Wings Won't Work
Written by Mignonne Gunasekara, Adapted by William Anthony
Illustrated by Kris Jones

An Introduction to Accessible Readers...

Our 'really readable' Accessible Readers have been specifically created to support the reading development of young readers with learning differences, such as dyslexia.

Our aim is to share our love of books with children, providing the same learning and developmental opportunities to every child.

INCREASED FONT SIZE AND SPACING improves readability and ensures text feels much less crowded.

OFF-WHITE BACKGROUNDS ON MATTE PAPER improves text contrast and avoids dazzling readers.

SIMPLIFIED PAGE LAYOUT reduces distractions and aids concentration.

CAREFULLY CRAFTED along guidelines set out in the British Dyslexia Association's Dyslexia-Friendly Style Guide.

Bernie Bee's Wings Won't Work

Written by Mignonne Gunasekara
Illustrated by Kris Jones

Bernie Bee was really excited. Today was the day that all the young bees were finally old enough to try to fly.

Their nurse, Miss Beedle, had gathered everyone by the entrance to the hive. She was letting them out in small groups.

Bernie huddled with her best friends, Billy, Bella and Brenda. The four of them had grown up together in the hive's nursery. They couldn't believe it was their time to fly already. They were very excited!

Being able to fly meant they could leave the hive for the first time. There was a whole world to explore! Before they knew it, Bernie's group was next to fly out of the hive.

"Are you ready?" asked Miss Beedle.

"I was born ready!" yelled Billy. With a hop he was up in the air.

"Wait for us!" Bella called. She flapped her wings and flew to join Billy. Brenda wasn't far behind.

"I'm flying!" squealed Brenda. "Let's go, Bernie!"

Bernie stepped up to take her turn while her friends watched. She closed her eyes and thought about flapping her wings.

Then Bernie leapt into the air... and fell straight back down to the floor. That wasn't supposed to happen.

Bernie looked up at her friends and their mouths were open in shock.

"Are you OK?" asked Miss Beedle.

"I think so," replied Bernie. "I don't know what happened."

"Try again, Bernie," said Miss Beedle. "It can sometimes take a few tries."

Bernie picked herself off the floor.

"OK, Miss Beedle," she said.

Bernie focused all her energy and tried again. It still wasn't enough to get her into the air.

"I can't do it," sniffled Bernie.

Miss Beedle comforted her.

"It's OK, Bernie," said Miss Beedle. "Let's take a break and try again in a minute."

Bernie sniffed and walked off to the side. She let the rest of the young bees have their turn.

Billy, Bella and Brenda slowly flew back down and walked over to her. They all started to speak at once.

"Are you OK?"

"What happened?"

"I don't know!" cried Bernie. "I... I don't think my wings work properly."

"Do you know for sure?" asked Bella.

"Maybe your third try will be lucky," said Brenda.

"Try one more time," said Billy.

"OK," said Bernie. "I'll try again."

Bernie tried to flap her wings so hard she thought she might burst, but nothing happened.

"Why can't I fly?" whispered Bernie. She felt like she was letting her friends down. They could be playing and exploring outside the hive, but they were stuck with her instead.

"You should all go back to flying," said Bernie. "You don't have to wait for me."

"Friends don't leave each other behind," said Brenda.

"No, really," she said over her shoulder. "I'll be OK. Go and have fun. I'll see you later."

Bernie ran around the corner and slumped against the wall.

What kind of a bee was a bee who couldn't fly? How would she play with her friends? What work could she do in the hive?

Bernie was snapped out of her sad thoughts by some yelling she could hear in the distance.

There was a massive panic by the hive entrance. Through the crowd, she saw her friends hovering just outside the entrance. Bernie was about to call out to them when she saw the wasps.

They were big. They were ugly. And they were attacking the hive.

Billy, Bella and Brenda were doing their best, but it looked like the wasps were winning. Bernie wished more than ever that she could fly. Her friends needed help!

Bernie wondered if anyone had told the mayor about the attack. Mayor Beety would know what to do about the wasps. Bernie turned and ran deep into the hive to tell her about what was happening.

Bernie burst into the mayor's office. She was drinking honey.

"Mayor Beety," gasped Bernie. "Come quickly! Wasps are attacking the hive!"

"Wasps?" said Mayor Beety, getting to her feet. "Where?"

"By the entrance!" replied Bernie.

"Not on my watch," said Mayor Beety.

She picked up a flower trumpet from her desk.

"Attention all fighter bees," Mayor Beety bellowed. "There is a wasp attack at the hive entrance."

Mayor Beety's words echoed loudly through the hive. There was silence, and then the buzzing started.

All the bees came together to fight the wasps. Bernie watched as bees flew past her, towards danger.

"Let's go, Bernie," said Mayor Beety. "Thank you for telling me about this."

"I want to do something to help," said Bernie. "But I can't fly."

"Don't worry, you've already helped," said Mayor Beety. "And I'm sure it will all be over soon."

Mayor Beety flew towards the wasps. Bernie followed on foot.

Bernie watched as the brave bees battled with the attacking wasps.

Even with everyone working together, the wasps still seemed to be winning. Bernie thought hard to come up with an idea. Then she remembered Mayor Beety's cup of honey...

"That's it!" said Bernie. "We can use what we do best to defeat the wasps!"

A few moments later, the fighting was stopped... by a blob of honey sailing through the air and smacking a wasp in the face.

Everyone turned to see where the honey came from.

There stood Bernie, with a catapult made of honeycomb and beeswax. She put more honey onto the catapult and let go. This time, it hit a wasp's wings.

The wasp couldn't beat its wings with all that honey coating them. Perfect!

The other bees understood what Bernie was trying to do.

"Quick," yelled Mayor Beety. "Everyone help her!"

Several bees rushed to scoop up honeycomb and beeswax.

They built catapults and started hurling honey at the wasps.

The honey was so thick and sticky that the wasps couldn't fly anymore. One by one, they crashed to the ground. The bees cheered. Bernie's idea had saved the day.

Bernie couldn't fly, but she thought on her feet and defeated the wasps. She was different to the other bees, but strong in her own way.

The hive was very proud of her, and Bernie finally felt like a proper bee.

Bernie Bee's Wings Won't Work: Quiz

1. How did Billy get up into the air?

2. Where were the wasps attacking the bees?

3. What was Mayor Beety drinking in her office?

4. What was Bernie's catapult made from?

5. Why did Bernie feel like she wasn't a proper bee? Have you ever felt that you're not good at something? What did you do?

Helpful Hints for Reading at Home

This 'really readable' Accessible Reader has been carefully written and designed to help children with learning differences whether they are reading in the classroom or at home. However, there are some extra ways in which you can help your child at home.

- Try to provide a quiet space for your child to read, with as few distractions as possible.

- Try to allow your child as much time as they need to decode the letters and words on the page.

- Reading with a learning difference can be frustrating and difficult. Try to let your child take short, managed breaks between reading sessions if they begin to feel frustrated.

- Build your child's confidence with positive praise and encouragement throughout.

- Your child's teacher, as well as many charities, can provide you with lots of tips and techniques to help your child read at home.